W9-CFH-585

Taizé: Songs for Prayer

Also available:
G-4956A Instrumental Edition
G-4956P Assembly/Choir Edition

GIA Publications, Inc., 7404 S. Mason Ave., Chicago, IL 60638
www.giamusic.com

Notice

The unauthorized copying of the **words** or **music** of this edition, for any reason whatsoever, is a direct violation of the copyright law for which the person responsible, as well as the institution he or she represents, is subject to prosecution. This includes hand copying, photocopying, even the making of just one copy. To do so is to deprive the persons whose names appear in this edition, as well as the publisher and its employees, of just income.

Perfect Bound ISBN: 1-57999-035-5
Spiral Bound ISBN: 1-57999-601-9

Taizé: Songs for Prayer
Copyright © 1998 Ateliers et Presses de Taizé (France)
International Copyright Secured   All Rights Reserved

This edition published through exclusive license agreement by
G.I.A. Publications, Inc.
7404 S. Mason Ave., Chicago, IL 60638 USA

Printed in U.S.A.

CONTENTS

D. Litanies

E. Eucharist

G. Psalms

H. Indexes

PRAYER AND SONG IN TAIZÉ

Many a visitor is astonished in observing what happens when the bells ring out, three times daily, across the hill of Taizé: one by one, various activities in the meetings come to a halt and all the participants beat a path, on their own or in little groups, to the church. During the busiest weeks of the year, when the Church of Reconciliation and its five extensions receive as many as 4000 to 6000 young adults, many even come early, as much as a half hour before common prayer begins, to "find a good place." Near the entrances, one sees young people holding signs with "silence" written in different languages, a reminder to enter quietly. At the entrance itself, copies of the song booklet are being distributed.

Once inside, it will take a moment to adjust one's eyes to the dimly lit interior. Soon one's gaze is drawn towards the front and the illuminated altar area with its icons, greenery, and many candles. The assembly is facing the altar, for the most part seated on the simply carpeted floor or kneeling, the others on benches arranged near the side walls. In the center, likewise facing forward, are the brothers of the Community in white robes, entering not all at once but one by one. After several moments, the bells grow quiet and another silence seems to permeate the church, more dense than before. The hill is now entirely still and the church is full.

To begin, a single voice: one of the brothers sings the first measure of an opening hymn to which, at once, the whole assembly joins in. If a spirit of silence pervades the church in Taizé, it is perhaps the sound of many voices singing together that most characterizes the prayer itself. Aside from Scripture readings and a benediction prayer, there are few spoken words.

After the introduction, a psalm is sung, then a Bible passage read in several languages—those present come from many countries, even different continents. A response, sung by a young child from the village of Taizé, interrupts briefly the flow of languages. A second response follows, this time a repetitive melodic motif, meditative in character, that leads into silence, a period of quiet that lasts some five to ten minutes. Afterwards, a litany of intercessory prayers is sung by several brother-cantors in turn with the assembly, which answers after each petition, "Kyrie eleison" (Lord, have mercy). There is a hymn, and then a simple benediction, read, again in several languages, by Brother Roger, the founder and prior of the Community. The structure is familiar, even if various elements that contribute to the prayer's contemplative quality may be new to some. In its essence, prayer in Taizé is no different than that which Christians of different traditions have practiced for ages in the form of the liturgy or prayer of hours. After the benediction prayer, another song follows and the brothers rise to leave the church, a signal—one might assume—that prayer has ended, until he or she notices that few persons, if any, are leaving. A careful look to the front reveals that, in fact, a part of the Community has stayed on and is continuing to animate the singing, now with the help of several young people. A second part to prayer unfolds, made up of simple melodies woven in succession into a kind of tapestry of continuous prayer. People trickle from the church, leaving when they wish. After evening prayer, many of the young people will stay on in prayer even late into the night. Several of the brothers remain available in the church for those who wish to speak with one of them and confide a personal question or difficulty.

Visitors often speak of being struck both by the beauty of prayer and the ease with which all present take part. These two attributes of prayer, which can sometimes seem contradictory, in Taizé are held together. Everywhere, whether it be in physical arrangements within the church or in the musical forms themselves, the underlying aim is to enter together into the mystery of God's presence. If one sees no director leading either choir or assembly and finds it hard even to locate the brother-cantors, if no announcements are made, it is for a reason. A "space" in which people can, as it were, find themselves able to pray depends, in great part, on an absence of outward distractions. When liturgy becomes a performance, either of a musical or a spiritual kind, when participants turn into observers, the very essence of prayer has been lost. The presence of children in the church—those who wish can sit in the middle, close to Brother Roger—is a wordless reminder that prayer is not a matter of method or expertise but trust. And to open the doors to trusting in God, there is perhaps nothing to replace the beauty of human voices joined in song. The beauty of many voices singing together can become an entry point onto what is beyond ordinary seeing and hearing, and provide a glimpse of what orthodox Christians like to call "heaven's joy on earth." An inner life awakens.

SINGING (and a few practical suggestions . . .)

Song is one of the most essential elements of worship. Short songs, repeated again and again, give it a meditative character. Using just a few words, they express a basic reality of faith, quickly grasped by the mind. As the words are sung over many times, this reality gradually penetrates the whole being. And these simple songs then enable us to keep on praying when we are alone, by day, by night, and sometimes in the silence of our hearts when we are at work.

If a song is begun spontaneously, the key is generally too low. A tuning fork or pitch pipe can help, or a guitar or recorder can give the first note or accompany the melody. A flute or organ or guitar can also begin a song by playing the melody or "simple melody" once as an introduction. This prepares all the voices to begin simultaneously. The person who begins the songs should make sure the tempo does not slow down too much, as this tends to happen when singing goes on for some time. Song practice should take place outside of the prayer itself, so that the atmosphere remains meditative. During the prayer, no one should direct the music; in this way everyone can face the cross, the icon or the altar.

OSTINATO REFRAINS, CANONS, ACCLAMATIONS

Today the name of Taizé has become familiar to many on account of its music and in particular the so-called songs from Taizé—the acclamations, ostinato refrains, and canons that do much to give the liturgy its unique character.

In this collection, an ostinato describes a musical unit sung in continuous repetition by all the people. Some pieces are meditative and calm in mood (for example, "Lord Jesus Christ," "Ubi caritas Deus ibi est"), others give an expression to a joy-filled praise (for example, "Laudate Dominum").

In the longer formulas, the assembly need only sing the melody, leaving the harmony to a choral group or a guitar or organ (for example, "In the Lord," "Tui Amoris"). Of course, everyone should feel free to sing their respective voice.

For the ostinatos of only two to four measures ("Lord God, You Love Us," "Veni Sancte Spiritus"), it will be more interesting for the assembly to sing all the vocal parts with the choir, since they are all very simple. They should be sung in a quiet, interior fashion so that the verses sung by a cantor can be clearly heard.

In all these songs, avoid mechanical and monotonous repetition. Variations in intensity are desirable: at times it will be calmer, and at other times more animated. A variety of soloists, too, is often desirable, moving between different vocal timbres and ranges (e.g., a soprano followed by a baritone).

Canons are another musical form very often used at Taizé. Their simple structure permits everyone to quickly take part in the prayer. The entries of each canon are indicated by a letter (A), (B). The assembly can be divided into two parts, male and female voices. For canons with up to four entries, a choir can enter with the third and fourth canon once the assembly is at ease with their two voices.

This collection of music from Taizé also includes the various elements of the Eucharist. The different pieces can be used separately or they can form the basis of an entire celebration. The acclamation "Send Forth Your Spirit, Lord" ("Mitte tuum Spiritum," #52) can be used in between the intercessions of the Eucharistic Prayer. The Amen (#47) can be sung at the end of the different prayers (Opening Prayer, Communion Prayer, Concluding Prayer).

The solos verses that are proposed in this collection are to be sung "over" their respective ostinato refrain. On the other hand, for the acclamations ("Alleluia," "Kyrie," "Veni lumen cordium," "Gospodi"), the solo verse is sung while the assembly hums a chord. In the case of a litany, it becomes possible to introduce written intercessions, which a soloist will improvise musically. The improvisation must remain short and simple, respecting the harmony of the acclamation. In the case of an Alleluia, the soloist can improvise on the verses of a psalm. The alleluias open our hearts to praise. A prayer can begin, for example, with the singing of five or six verses of a psalm, with the assembly responding after each verse with "alleluia."

Taizé: Songs for Prayer

1. ALL YOU WHO PASS THIS WAY

(Matthew 27:46) D.C.

3. My God, my God, why have you a - ban - doned me?

(Luke 23:43) D.C.

4. To - day you will be with me in par - a - dise.

(Luke 23:46) D.C.

5. Fa - ther, — in - to your hands I com - mend my spir - it.

2. BE NOT AFRAID

Nebojte se

Be not a-fraid, sing out for joy! Christ is ris-en, al-le-lu - ia!
Ne-boj-te se, ra-duj-te se! Kris-tus slav-ný ví-téz z hro-bu vstal.

Be not a-fraid, sing out for joy! Christ is ris-en, al-le-lu - ia!
Ne-boj-te se, ra-duj-te se! Kris-tus slav-ný ví-téz z hro-bu vstal.

3. BLESS THE LORD

♩ = 72
(Psalm 103:1)

Bless the Lord, my soul, and bless God's ho - ly name.

Bless the Lord, my soul, who leads me in - to life.

6

Verses From Psalm (102) 103 *(Superimposed on ostinato chorale)*

1. For - get not my soul all God's good deeds.

2. The Lord is for - give - ness and re - deems our life from the grave.

3. The Lord is com - pas - sion - ate and gra - cious, a - bound - ing in love.

4. It is God who for - gives all your guilt, who heals ev - 'ry - one of your ills, who re - deems your life from the grave, who crowns you with love and com - pas - sion.

5. The Lord is com - pas - sion and love, the Lord is pa - tient and rich in mer - cy. God does not treat us ac - cord - ing to our sins nor re - pay us ac - cord - ing to our faults.

6. As a Fa - ther has com - pas - sion on his chil - dren, the Lord has mer - cy on those who re - vere him; for God knows of what we are made, and re - mem - bers that we are dust.

*Choose either part.

7. As the heav- ens are high a- bove the earth, so is

God's way a- bove our way, so is God's love for us.

8. All your works are ho- ly, for you are our God;

you bring jus- tice to the op- pressed.

9. From ev- er- last- ing to ev- er- last- ing your love is for

those who re- vere you.

8

4. CHRISTUS RESURREXIT
Jesus Christ Is Risen

O—————

Chri-stus re - sur-re-xit, Chri-stus re - sur-re-xit.
Je - sus Christ is ris- en, Je - sus Christ is ris- en!

O—————

Al - le-lu - ia, al-le-lu - ia!
Al - le-lu - ia, al-le-lu - ia!

Verses From Psalm (117) 118 *(Superimposed on ostinato chorale)*
Cantor

1. Give thanks to the Lord for he is— good, for God's love

has no end. 2. I called to the Lord in my dis-tress,

God an-swered me, and freed me. 3. The Lord is at my side;

I do not fear. What can an-y-one do a-gainst me?

4. O-pen to me the gates of ho-li-ness:

I will en-ter and I will give thanks. 5. I will thank you for

you have heard my call. You, O Lord, are my Sav-ior.

6. This is the day the Lord has made, let us re-joice and

let us be glad. 7. This is the day the Lord has made,

let us re-joice and be glad, al-le-lu-ia! 8. The

Lord is my strength, God is my song. God has be-come my sal-

va-tion. 9. Give thanks to the Lord for

he is good; God's love en-dures for ev-er.

5. DE NOCHE IREMOS
By Night, We Hasten

De no - che i - re - mos, de no - che que pa - ra en - con - trar la
By night, we has - ten, in dark - ness, to search for liv - ing

fuen - te, só - lo la sed nos a - lum - bra,
wa - ter, on - ly our thirst leads us on - wards,

só - lo la sed nos a - lum - bra. De
on - ly our thirst leads us on - wards. By

Verses *(Superimposed on ostinato chorale)*

Cantor

1. We will go by night.

To find the source, thirst is our on - ly light.

(Psalm 42:2)

2. My soul— thirsts for God, the God of life.

The Lord is my Sav - ior and my God.

(Psalm 42:6)

3. Why are you cast down, O my soul? Hope in God;

for I shall praise him a - gain, my help and my God.

(Psalm 42:8)

4. By day the Lord com - mands his stead - fast love, and at

night his song is with me, a prayer to the God of my life.

This page is blank in order to avoid excessive page turns.

6. DONA NOBIS PACEM
(Give us peace of heart)

14

7. EAT THIS BREAD
Jesus Christ, Bread of Life

May be sung as an ostinato by omitting verses.

Eat this bread, drink this cup, come to him and nev-er be hun-gry.
Je-sus Christ, bread of life, those who come to you will not hun-ger.

Eat this bread, drink this cup, trust in him and you will not thirst.
Je-sus Christ, Ris-en Lord, those who trust in you will not thirst.

Verses From John 6

Choose either part.

8. IN GOD ALONE MY SOUL

Mon âme se repose

In God a-lone my soul can find rest and peace, in
Mon â-me se re-po-se en paix sur Dieu seul: de

God my peace and joy. On-ly in God my
lui vient mon sa-lut. Oui, sur Dieu seul mon

Verses From Psalm 62 *(Superimposed on ostinato chorale)*

Cantor

1. For God a-lone my soul waits in si-lence; from God comes my sal -

va - tion. God a-lone is my rock and my sal-va - tion.

2. For God a - lone I wait in si - lence;

for my hope is in God.

3. God a-lone is my rock, my sal-va - tion, God is my for -

tress; I shall not be shak - en.

9. IN TE CONFIDO
Christ of Compassion

Verses From Psalm 25 *(Superimposed on ostinato chorale)*

Cantor

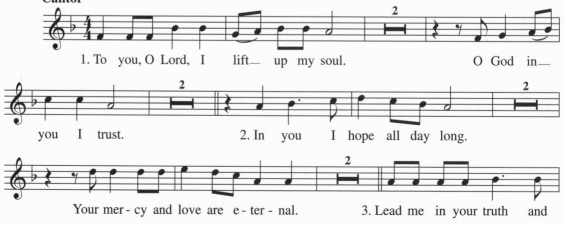

1. To you, O Lord, I lift up my soul. O God in you I trust.

2. In you I hope all day long. Your mer-cy and love are e-ter-nal.

3. Lead me in your truth and

teach me, O Lord. For you are the God of my sal-va-tion.

4. Good and up-right is the Lord our God. The Lord teach-es the hum-ble his way.

5. All the paths of the Lord are stead-fast love, mer-cy and faith-ful-ness.

6. The Lord turns to me and shows me— mer-cy. The Lord calms the troub-les of my heart.

7. My eyes are turned t'ward the Lord. For the Lord frees my feet from the snare.

8. You hold me Lord, by my right hand. Your pres-ence nev-er leaves me, Lord.

9. Who have I in heav-en but you? On earth there is noth-ing I de-sire more than you.

10. My flesh and heart may fail, but you, my heart's rock, God for-ev-er.

Choose either part.

10. IN THE LORD I'LL BE EVER THANKFUL

El Senyor és la meva força

(Isaiah 12:2)

In the Lord I'll be ev - er thank - ful, in the Lord I will re -
El Se - nyor és la me - va for - ça, el Se - nyor el me - u

joice! Look to God, do not be a - fraid. Lift up your voic - es, the Lord is
cant. Ell m'ha es - tat la sal - va - ci - ó. En ell con - fi - o i no tinc

near; lift up your voic - es, the Lord is near. In the
por. En ell con - fi - o i no tinc por. El Se -

Verses *(Superimposed on ostinato chorale)*

Cantor   (Isaiah 12:2)

1. You are my sal - va - tion; I trust in you. I shall not be a- fraid, you are my strength; you are my song.

(Psalm 18:2)

2. The Lord is my rock. The Lord is my for-tress. My God, you are my ref - uge and my shield.

(Psalm 18:3)

3. I call up-on the Lord God who is wor-thy of praise. The Lord shall save_____ me.

(Isaiah 12:5)

4. My soul shall sing to you; you have done won - drous things, O God. Let this be known, let this be known through - out the world.

(Isaiah 12:3-4)

5. With joy you will draw wa - ter at the foun - tain of sal - va - tion. Give thanks to the Lord. Pro - claim God's name.

22

11. JESUS, REMEMBER ME

(Luke 23:42)

Jesus, remember me when you come into your kingdom.

Jesus, remember me when you come into your kingdom.

12. LAUDATE DOMINUM

Sing, Praise and Bless the Lord

24

Verses *(Superimposed on ostinato chorale)*

Cantor (Psalm 117)

1. Praise the Lord, all you na-tions; praise him, all you peo-ples; al - le - lu - ia. Strong is his love and mer - cy, God is faith-ful for ev - er, al - le - lu - ia.

(Psalm 150:6)

2. Al - le - lu - ia, al - le - lu - ia, let ev - 'ry-thing liv - ing give praise to the Lord. Al - le - praise to the Lord.

(Psalm 47:1)

3. Let the earth shout to God with joy, al - le - lu - ia, al - le - lu - ia. Let the earth wor - ship with sounds of glad - ness, al - le - lu - ia, al - le - lu - ia.

(Psalm 100:2-3)

4. We come be - fore you with joy - ful songs, al - le - lu - ia, al - le - lu - ia. You are our God, you have made us, al - le - lu - ia, al - le - lu - ia, al - le - lu - ia.

*Choose either part.

(Psalm 100:3)

5. You— are— our God, we be - long to— you, al - le - lu -
ia, al - le - lu - ia. We are— your peo - ple, the
sheep of your flock, al - le - lu - ia, al - le - lu - ia.

(Psalm 100:4)

6. Let— us then en - ter your gates with— thanks - giv - ing, al - le - lu -
ia, al - le - lu - ia. Let us give thanks and—
praise your— name, al - le - lu - ia, al - le - lu - ia.

(Psalm 100:5)

7. For you— are— good and your love lasts for ev - er, al - le - lu -
ia, al - le - lu - ia. Your faith - ful - ness lasts from age to—
age, al - le - lu - ia, al - le - lu - ia.

26

13. LET US SING TO THE LORD
Bénissez le Seigneur

Let us sing to the Lord!
Bé-nis-sez le Sei-gneur!

Let us sing to the
Bé-nis-sez le Sei-

O_____

O_____

Lord!
gneur!

Let us sing to the Lord! Let us sing to the Lord!
Bé-nis-sez le Sei-gneur, bé-nis-sez le Sei-gneur!

O_____

Let us sing to the Lord! Let us sing to the Lord!
Bé-nis-sez le Sei-gneur, bé-nis-sez le Sei-gneur!

7. Praised be Christ, he is our hope. He is the joy of our hearts.

Com - pas - sion - ate and gra - cious is our God.

8. The Lord o - pens up a way, and leads us on

paths of___ life. The earth is full of God's love.

(1 John 4:19)

9. Christ is al - ways with us, and loves us be - fore we love

him. God's love will nev - er pass a - way.

(Luke 1:46-47, 49)

10. My soul glo - ri - fies the Lord. My spir - it re - joic - es in

God. The Lord has done won - ders for me.

11. The glo - ry of the Lord fills the earth. Let all peo - ple bless God's_

name. Let ev - 'ry - thing that breathes bless the Lord.

(Psalm 95:1-2)

12. Sing a - loud to the Lord. Praise our God for his

won - der - ful deeds. Shout for joy to our God.

14. LORD GOD, YOU LOVE US
Toi, tu nous aimes

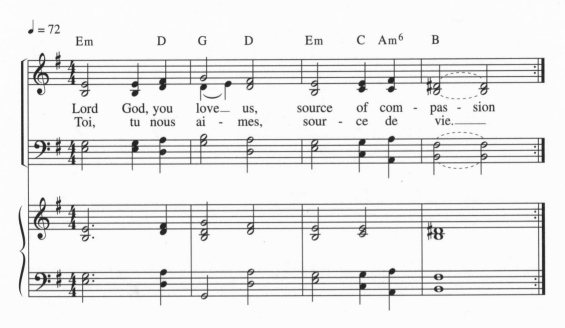

Lord God, you love us, source of com-pas-sion
Toi, tu nous ai-mes, sour-ce de vie.

Verses A prayer by Brother Roger of Taizé *(Superimposed on ostinato chorale)*

Cantor

1. Lord Christ, if we had faith e-nough to move moun-tains but were with-out liv-ing char-i-ty, what would we be? You love us. You love us.

2. With-out your Spir - it who dwells in our hearts, what would we be? You love us. You love us.

3. Tak - ing ev - 'ry-thing up - on your-self,

you o - pen a way for us t'wards faith, t'wards trust in God,

who— wants nei - ther suf- f'ring nor hu - man dis - tress.

4. Spir - it of the Ris- en Christ, Spir - it of com- pas- sion,

Spir - it of praise, your love for each one of us will

nev - er go a - way, will nev - er go a - way.

15. LORD JESUS CHRIST

Jésus le Christ

Lord Je - sus Christ, your light shines with - in us.
Jé - sus le Christ, lu - mière in - té - rieu - re,

Let not my doubts nor my dark-ness speak to me. Lord Je - sus Christ, your
ne lais - se pas mes té - nè - bres me par - ler. Jé - sus le Christ, lu -

light shines with-in us. Let my heart al - ways wel-come your love.
mière in - té - rieu - re, don - ne - moi d'ac-cueil - lir ton a - mour.

Verses From Psalm 139 *(Superimposed on ostinato chorale)*

1. Lord, you have searched me and known me; you know when I sit down, when I rise up. You are ac-quaint-ed with all my ways.

2. If I take the wings of the morn-ing, and set-tle at the farth-est lim-its of the sea, e-ven there your hand shall hold me fast.

3. If I say, "Let the dark-ness cov-er me," e-ven the dark-ness is not dark to you, and night is as bright as the day.

4. Search me, God, and know my heart and lead me in the ev-er-last-ing way.

*Choose either part.

16. NUNC DIMITTIS
Let Your Servant Now Go in Peace

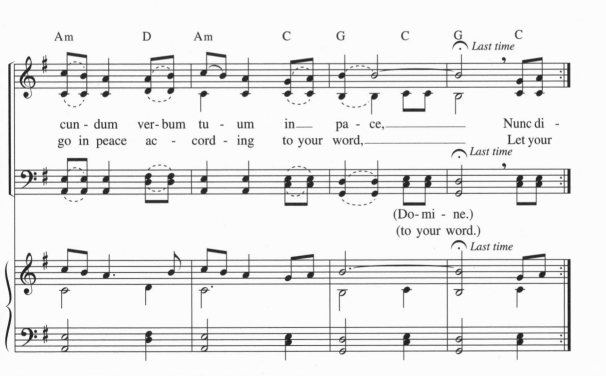

17. OCULI NOSTRI
Our Eyes are Turned

18. OUR DARKNESS

La ténèbre

(Psalm 139:12)

Our_ dark-ness is nev-er dark-ness in your sight: the
La té - nè - bre n'est point té - nè - bre de-vant toi: la

deep - est night is clear as the day - light. Our_
nuit com - me le jour est lu - miè - re. La té -

19. OUR SOUL IS WAITING

Notre âme attend le Seigneur

Our soul is wait-ing for God. Our hearts find joy — in the Lord.
Notre âme at-tend le Sei-gneur. En lui la joie de no-tre cœur.

Verses *(Cantor)*

Verses B *(Superimposed on second half of ostinato chorale)*

Cantor (Psalm 130:5) B

1. My soul is wait-ing for the Lord; I count on God's word.

B (Psalm 52:10)

2. I trust in the good-ness of God for ev - er and ev - er.

B (Psalm 16:1)

3. Keep me, O God, I take ref - uge in you.

(Psalm 59:10) B

4. O my Strength, it is you to whom I turn. You who show me love.

B (Psalm 59:16)

5. As for me I will sing of your strength and each morn-ing ac-claim your love.

B (Psalm 13:5)

6. I trust in your mer-ci-ful love. My heart re - joic - es in you.

(Isaiah 12:2) B

7. The Lord is my strength, my song, my sal - va - tion: in

God I trust, I'm not a - fraid.

(Isaiah 12:4) B

8. Give thanks to the Lord, pro - claim God's deeds.

Cry out for joy and glad - ness.

*Choose either part.

38

20. PSALLITE DEO
This Is the Day

Verses From Psalm (97) 98:1-6 and Psalm (117) 118:7-12

*Choose either part.

trum - pets and the sound of the horn, ac- claim the Lord, your God.

5. Let the sea and all with-in it, thun-der; the world and

all its— peo-ples. 6. Let the riv - ers clap their hands

and the hills sing out their joy. 7. Give thanks to the Lord, for

he is good, for God's love en- dures for ev- er.

8. Let those who wor - ship God pro- claim: God's love en-dures for

ev - er. 9. In— my dis-tress I called to the Lord.

God heard my voice and set me free. 10. God is my strength, God is my song;

the Lord has be-come my sav - ior. 11. I shall not die,

I shall live. I shall pro-claim the mar-vels of the Lord.

12. This is the day the Lord has made; let us re-joice and be glad!

13. Al - le - lu-ia, al - le - lu - ia. A - men! A - men!

40

21. SING TO GOD
Singt dem Herrn

Sing to God with joy-ful hearts. Praise the Lord for
Singt dem Herrn ein neu-es Lied. Lob-singt ihm

ev-er-more, praise the Lord for ev-er-more.
al-le-zeit, lob-singt ihm al-le-zeit!

Verses *(Cantor) Keyboard doubles voices.*

Verses B *(Superimposed on second part of ostinato chorale)*

Cantor B *(Psalm 96:2)*

1. Sing to the Lord all ___ the earth,

sing and bless God's ho - ly name.

B *(Psalm 98:1)*

2. Sing a new song to the Lord,

*

for God has done mar - vel - ous deeds.

(Psalm 98:2) B

3. The Lord has made known his sal - va -

tion for all peo - ples to be - hold.

(Psalm 98:3) B

4. The Lord has re - mem - bered his faith - ful - ness, his

stead - fast love for all peo - ples.

(Psalm 98:4) B

5. Make a joy - ful noise to the Lord!

Break forth in - to songs of praise!

*Choose either part.

42

(Psalm 98:5-6) B

6. Sing prais - es to the Lord___ with sounds___ of mu - sic, with trum - pet and horn, re - joice in the Lord.

B (Psalm 98:7-8)

7. Let the sea roar, let the floods clap their hands, and the hills sing to - geth - er for joy in the Lord.

(Psalm 97:6) B

8. The heav - ens pro - claim the Lord's right - eous - ness and all peo - ples be - hold___ his glo - ry.

(Psalm 98:8-9) B

9. Let the heav - ens re - joice and the earth be glad, for the Lord is com - ing, God is com - ing.

22. SING TO THE LORD

Lobe den Herrn

23. SURREXIT CHRISTUS
The Lord Is Risen

Surrexit Christus, alleluia!
The Lord is risen, alleluia!

Cantate Domino, alleluia!
Sing out and praise the Lord, alleluia!

Verses From Daniel 3:58-87 and Psalm 117:6-8 *(Superimposed on ostinato chorale)*

Cantor

1. All you heav-ens, bless the Lord. Stars of the heav-ens,
bless the Lord. 2. Sun and moon, bless the Lord;

and you, night and day, bless the Lord.

3. Frost and cold, bless the Lord. Ice and snow,

bless the Lord. 4. Fire and heat, bless the Lord;

and you, light and dark - ness, bless the Lord.

5. Spir - its and souls of the just, bless the Lord.

Saints and the hum - ble heart-ed, bless the Lord.

6. Give thanks to the Lord, for he is good,

for God's love has no end.

7. The Lord is my strength, the Lord is my song; God has been my

Sav - ior. 8. I shall not die, I shall live.

I shall live and re - count God's deeds.

Choose either part.

24. TUI AMORIS IGNEM
Holy Spirit, Come to Us

47

Verses *(Superimposed on ostinato chorale)*

Cantor

1. Je-sus said, "I give you a new com-mand-ment: Love one an-oth-er just as I have loved you."

2. Je-sus said, "It is by your love for one an-oth-er, that ev-'ry one will rec-og-nize you as my dis-ci-ples."

3. Je-sus said, "No one has great-er love than this: to lay down one's life for those one loves."

4. We know love by this, that Christ laid down his life for us.

5. This is love: it is not we who have loved God but God who loved us.

6. God is love, and those who a-bide in love a-bide in God and God in them.

*Choose either part.

25. UBI CARITAS DEUS IBI EST
Where There Is Charity

Verses From John 3:16-17 and 1 John 4:7-10 *(Superimposed on ostinato chorale)*

Cantor

1. God___ so loved___ the world___ that he gave his on - ly___ Son___ so that all who be - lieve in him may not per - ish___ but may have e - ter - nal___ life.___

2. God did not send the Son___ in - to the world to con - demn___ the world but in or - der that the world___ might___ be saved through___ him.___

3. Let us love one an - oth - er be-cause love___ is from___ God; ev - 'ry - one who loves___ is___ born of God___ and knows God.___

4. God's love was re - vealed a - mong us___ in this way:___ ___ God sent his Son in - to the

50

world___ so that we might live___ through him.___

5. In___ this___ is love,___ not that we_ loved

God but that God, first,___ loved___

___ us. No___ one___ has ev - er seen_

God. If we love one an - oth - er, God_ lives in

us and his love is made per - fect in___ us.

6. We have seen and do tes - ti - fy that___ the

Fa - ther has_ sent his Son,___ has sent his Son as

Sav - ior,___ as_ Sav - ior of the world.___

7. We have known and be - lieve___ the love that

God has for us. God___ is love and those who a -

bide_ in___ love, a - bide in God and God a - bides in them.

26. VENI CREATOR SPIRITUS

Choose either part.

3. You our on - ly Com - fort - er. Come, give us your

peace. Guide our steps with your light.

4. When in stress you sup - port us, in trials you give us

strength, con - so - la - tion in the midst of grief.

5. E - ter-nal light,_____ vis - it the hearts you have cre -

at - ed and fill our in - ner-most be - ing. Heal our

wounds and re - new our__ strength, quench our deep - est thirst. Fill us

with your grace. Come, fill us with your gifts.

6. Give us__ com - fort. Give us life. Give us joy, give us

joy that nev - er ends. Come! Come! Come, Ho - ly Spir - it!

7. Al - le - lu - ia. Al - le - lu - ia. A - men.

27. VENI LUMEN

Come Holy Spirit, Comforter

O_____

Veni Cre - a - tor
Come Ho - ly Spir - it,

Spi - ri - tus.
Com - fort - er.

O_____

Ve - ni lu - men
Come Cre - a - tor

cor - di - um, ve - ni___ lu - men cor - di - um.
Spir - it! Come! Come and___ lead us with__ your light!

54

Verses *(Superimposed on ostinato chorale)*

Cantor (Psalm 104:30)

1. Send forth your Spir - it, Lord, and re-new the face of the earth.

2. Come, Ho - ly Spir - it, come, Fa - ther of the poor.

3. Come, gen - er - ous Spir - it, come, come, light of our hearts.

4. You are our on - ly Com - fort - er, peace of the soul.

5. In troub - le you are our strength and in our sad - ness, con - so - la - tion.

6. Send rain up - on our dry ground. Heal our wound-ed souls.

7. Grant us all your gifts. Give us ev - er - last - ing joy.

8. Ho - ly— Spir - it, Well-spring of life, you are love, joy and peace.

9. In - flame our wait - ing hearts. Re - new us in— your love.

*Choose either part.

28. VENI SANCTE SPIRITUS

Holy Spirit, Come to Us

To begin this ostinato, the voices enter one at a time in the following order: Bass, Alto, Soprano, Tenor. Sing the ostinato twice before adding the next voice.

Ve - ni San - cte Spi - ri - tus.___
Ho - ly Spir - it, come to us.___

Verses *As the ostinato continues, vocal and instrumental verses are sung or played as desired with some space always left between the verses (after the cantor's "Veni Sancte Spiritus").*

Cantor

1. Come, Ho - ly Spir - it,___ from heav - en shine___ forth with your glo - rious light. Ve - ni San - cte Spi - ri - tus.___

2. Come, Fa - ther___ of the poor, come, gen - er - ous Spir - it,___ come, light of our hearts.___ Ve - ni San - cte Spi - ri - tus.___

3. Come from the four winds, O Spir - it, come breath of God;___ dis - perse the shad - ows o - ver us, re - new and strength - en your peo - ple.___

Ve - ni San - cte Spi - ri - tus.___ 4. Most

kind - ly warm - ing light! En - ter the in - most depths of our hearts, for

we are faith-ful to you. With-out your pres-ence, we have noth-ing wor-thy

noth - ing pure. Ve - ni San - cte Spi - ri - tus.___

5. You are our on - ly com-fort-er,___ peace___ of the

soul. In the heat you shade us; in our la-bor___ you re -

fresh us,___ and in troub-le, you are our strength.

Ve - ni San - cte Spi - ri - tus.___ 6. On

all who put their trust in you, and re-ceive you in faith,

show-er all your gifts. Grant that they may grow in you___ and

per - se-vere to the end, give them last-ing joy. Ve-ni San-cte Spi-ri-tus.___

29. VENITE, EXULTEMUS DOMINO

O Come and Let Us Sing To God

♩ = 84

Ve - ni - te, e - xul - te - mus Do - mi - no, ve -
O come and let us sing to God,— our hope. God's

ni - te, a - do - re - mus. Ve - ni - te, e - xul - te - mus
mer - cy is for ev - er. O come and let us sing to

Do - mi - no, ve - ni - te, a - do - re - mus. Ve-
God,— our hope. God's mer - cy is for ev - er. O

Last time

30. WAIT FOR THE LORD

Verses *(Superimposed on ostinato chorale)*

Cantor (Isaiah 40:3)

1. Pre-pare the way for the Lord. Make a straight path for God.

Pre - pare the way for the Lord.

(Phil. 4:4-5, and Psalm 70:4)

2. Re-joice in the Lord al-ways: God is at hand.

Joy and glad - ness for all who seek the Lord.

(Isaiah 40:5)

3. The glo - ry of the Lord shall be re -

vealed. All the earth will see the Lord.

(Psalm 38:15)

4. I wait - ed for the Lord. God heard my cry.

(Psalm 123:2)

5. Our eyes are fixed on the Lord, our

(Matthew 6:33, 7:7)

God. 6. Seek first the king-dom of

God. Seek and you shall find.

(Psalm 86:11)

7. O Lord, show us your way. Guide us in your truth.

Choose either part.

31. WITH YOU, O LORD

(Psalm 36:10)

With you, O Lord, is life in all its full - ness, and in your light we shall see true light. With you, O Lord, is life in all its full-ness, and in your light we shall see true light.

Verses *(Superimposed on ostinato chorale)*

Choose either part.

This page is blank in order to avoid excessive page turns.

32. YOUR WORD, O LORD

C'est toi ma lampe

(Psalm 119:105)

Your word, O Lord, is a light. My God, en-light-en my dark-ness. O Lord, my God, en-light-en my dark-ness. O Lord, my God, en-light-en my dark-ness. Your

C'est toi ma lam-pe, Sei-gneur. Mon Dieu é-clai-re ma té-nè-bre. Sei-gneur, mon Dieu, é-clai-re ma té-nè-bre. Sei-gneur, mon Dieu, é-clai-re ma té-nè-bre. C'est

33. DA PACEM, DOMINE

Grant Us Your Peace, O Lord

Canon

Da pa-cem, Do - mi - ne, da pa-cem,
Grant us your peace, O Lord, grant us your

O Chri - ste, in di - e - bus no - stris.
peace, O Lord, may it fill all our days.

Coda

A - men. A - men. A - men.

The Ⓑ and Ⓓ entrances in the canon are sung a fourth lower.

Canon fully notated

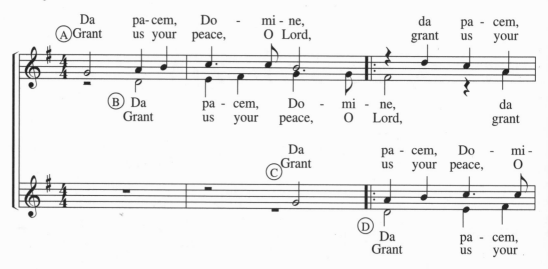

Keyboard

34. GLORIA II

Four canons on the same harmonic pattern using the same accompaniments.

1. Gloria II

Glo-ri-a, glo-ri-a, in ex-cel-sis De-o, glo-ri-a, glo-ri-a, al-le-lu-ia!

Et in ter-ra pax ho - mi - ni-bus bo-næ vo-lun-ta - tis.

2. Come and Pray In Us

Come and pray in us, Ho - ly Spir-it, come and pray in us,
Vie - ni, Spi-ri-to cre - a-to-re, vie - ni, vie - ni,

come and vis-it us, Ho - ly Spir-it, Spir-it come, Spir-it come.
vie - ni, Spi-ri-to cre - a-to-re, vie - ni, vie - ni!

3. Cantate Domino

Can - ta-te Do - mi - no. Al-le-lu-ia, al-le-
Sing— prais-es to the Lord. Al-le-lu-ia, al-le-

lu - ia! Ju - bi-la - te De - o.
lu - ia! Sing in joy and glad - ness.

4. Veni Creator Spiritus

Ve - ni Cre - a-tor, ve - ni Cre - a-tor,
Come, Cre - a - tor, Ho - ly Spir - it,

ve - ni Cre - a - tor Spi-ri - tus.
come Cre - a - tor Spir - it, come!

Accompaniments

Keyboard or Instruments

♩ = 100   Cm G/B Cm   Fm/A♭   G

I

II

pedal

Solo or Small Choir *(superimposed on the canons)*

Ⓐ

Sur - re - xit Chri-stus ho - di - e!

Ⓑ

Glo - ri - a! Glo - ri - a! Glo - ri - a, al-le - lu - ia!

Tenor and Soprano Solo

Ⓐ

Tenor: Al-le-lu - ia, al-le-lu - ia, al-le-lu-ia, al-le-lu -

Ⓑ ia! Al-le-lu - ia, al-le-lu-ia! Ⓒ

Soprano: Al-le-lu - ia, al-le-lu -

Ⓓ

ia, al-le-lu-ia, al-le-lu - ia! Al-le-lu - ia, al-le-lu-ia!

35. JUBILATE CŒLI

Heavens Sing with Gladness

Canon

Ju - bi - la - te cœ - li, ju - bi - la - te mun - di,
Heav - ens _ sing with glad - ness; earth sing out re - joic - ing:

(re.) Ju - bi - la - te cœ - li, ju - bi - la - te
(dead.) Heav-ens sing with glad - ness; earth sing out re -

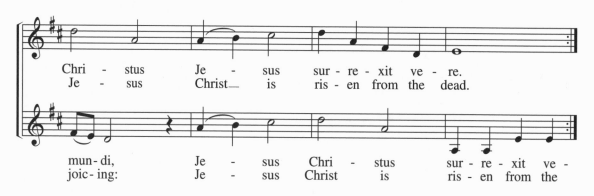

Chri - stus Je - sus sur - re - xit ve - re.
Je - sus Christ _ is ris - en from the dead.

mun - di, Je - sus Chri - stus sur - re - xit ve -
joic - ing: Je - sus Christ is ris - en from the

Coda

Solo Ⓐ   *2nd canon melody* Ⓐ1   *Tutti*

A - men, a - men! A - men!

Keyboard

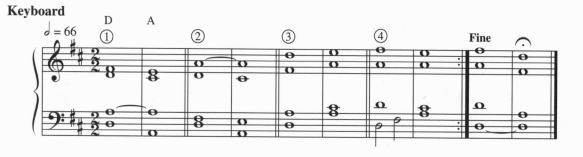

① D A ② ③ ④ **Fine**

36. SURREXIT DOMINUS VERE II

Jesus, the Lord, Is Risen

Canon

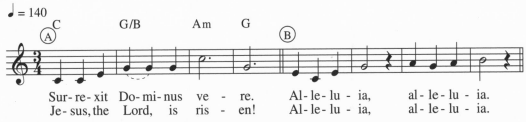

Sur-re-xit Do-mi-nus ve - re. Al-le-lu - ia, al-le-lu - ia.
Je-sus, the Lord, is ris - en! Al-le-lu - ia, al-le-lu - ia.

Sur-re-xit Chri-stus ho-di - e. Al-le-lu - ia, al-le-lu - ia.
Je-sus, the Lord, is ris-en to-day! Al-le-lu - ia, al-le-lu - ia.

Keyboard

37. ALLELUIA

Alleluia 1

Soprano ad lib.

Al - le - lu - ia, al - le - lu - ia, al - le - lu - ia, al - le - lu - ia!

Cantor

Al - le - lu - ia.

Alleluia 8

Al - le - lu - ia, al - le - lu - ia.

Al - le - lu - ia, al - le - lu - ia, al - le - lu - ia, al - le - lu - ia!

Alleluia 10

Al - le - lu - ia!

Al - le - lu - ia, al - le - lu - ia, al - le - lu - ia!

Al - le - lu - ia!

Al - le - lu - ia, al - le - lu - ia, al - le - lu - ia!

Alleluia 14

Alleluia 15

Alleluia 16

Alleluia 17

Alleluia 18

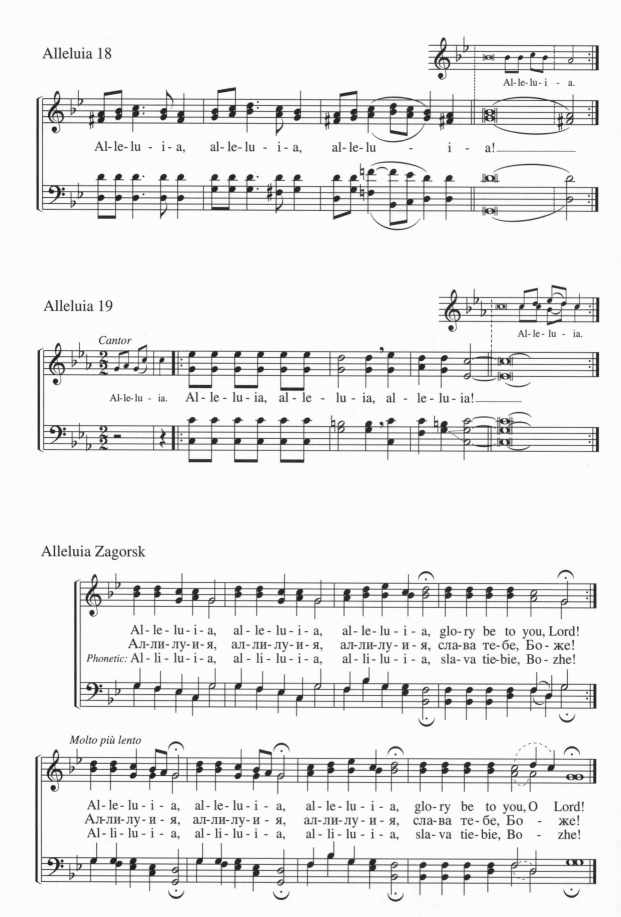

Al-le-lu-i - a.

Al-le-lu-i - a, al-le-lu-i - a, al-le-lu - i - a!____

Alleluia 19

Cantor

Al-le-lu-i - a.

Al - le-lu - ia. Al-le-lu - ia, al-le - lu - ia, al - le-lu - ia!____

Alleluia Zagorsk

Al-le-lu-i - a, al-le-lu-i - a, al-le-lu-i - a, glo-ry be to you, Lord!
Ал-ли-лу-и - я, ал-ли-лу-и - я, ал-ли-лу-и - я, сла-ва те-бе, Бо - же!
Phonetic: Al - li-lu-i - a, al - li-lu-i - a, al - li-lu-i - a, sla-va tie-bie, Bo - zhe!

Molto più lento

Al-le-lu-i - a, al-le-lu-i - a, al-le-lu-i - a, glo-ry be to you, O Lord!
Ал-ли-лу-и - я, ал-ли-лу-и - я, ал-ли-лу-и - я, сла-ва те-бе, Бо - же!
Al - li-lu-i - a, al - li-lu-i - a, al - li-lu-i - a, sla-va tie-bie, Bo - zhe!

38. ADORAMUS TE, O CHRISTE

74

*Choose either part.

39. CHRISTE JESU LUMEN CORDIUM

Chri- ste Je- su lu- men cor- di- um lau- da- bo te.____

40. EXAUDI NOS
Lord, Hear Our Prayer

Ex- au- di nos. Ex- au- di nos.____
Lord, hear our prayer, Lord, hear our prayer.____

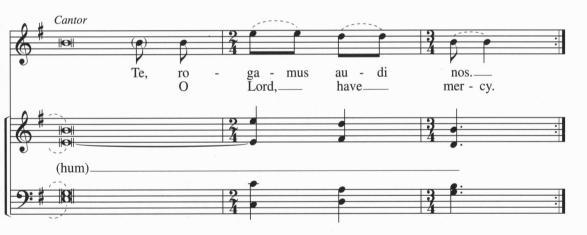

Cantor

Te, ro- ga- mus au- di nos.____
O Lord,____ have____ mer- cy.

(hum)____

41. GOSPODI
(Lord, have mercy.)

Gospodi A

Gos- po- di po- mi- lui.
Гос- по- ди по- ми- луй.

Gospodi B

Gos - po - di po - mi - lui, Gos - po - di po - mi - lui.
Гос - по-ди по - ми - луй, Гос - по-ди по - ми - луй.

Gospodi C

Gos - po - di po - mi - lui.
Гос - по-ди по-ми - луй.

Gospodi E

Gos - po - di po - mi - lui, Gos - po - di po - mi - lui.
Гос - по-ди по - ми - луй, Гос - по-ди по-ми - луй.

Gospodi F

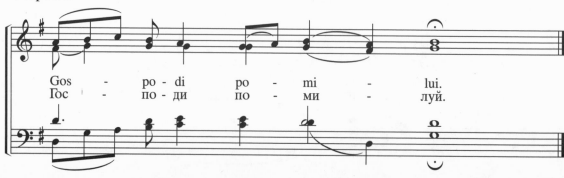

Gos - po - di po - mi - lui.
Гос - по-ди по - ми - луй.

42. KYRIE ELEISON

43. Maranatha! Alleluia! I

* ♩. *remains consistent.*

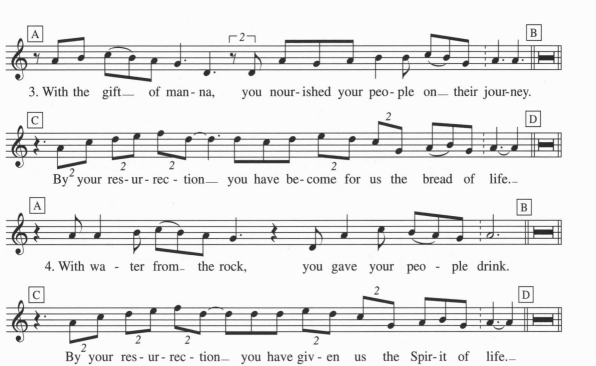

3. With the gift— of man - na, you nour - ished your peo - ple on— their jour - ney.

By² your res - ur - rec - tion— you have be - come for us the bread of life._

4. With wa - ter from— the rock, you gave your peo - ple drink.

By² your res - ur - rec - tion— you have giv - en us the Spir - it of life._

44. VENI LUMEN CORDIUM I
Come, Creator Spirit, Come

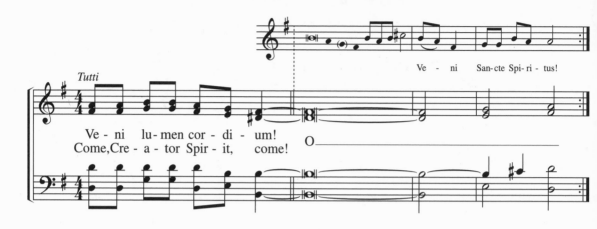

45. VENI LUMEN CORDIUM II
Come, Lord, Light of Our Hearts

EUCHARIST
46. KYRIE ELEISON, CHRISTE ELEISON

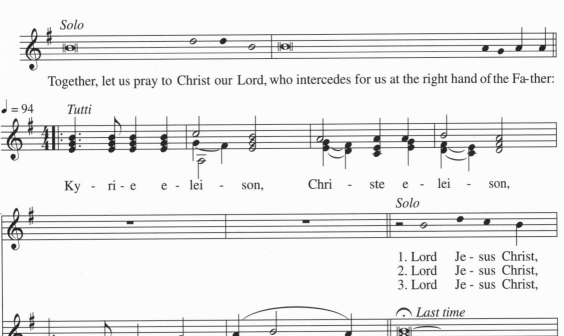

Together, let us pray to Christ our Lord, who intercedes for us at the right hand of the Fa-ther:

Ky - ri - e e - lei - son, Chri - ste e - lei - son,

1. Lord Je - sus Christ,
2. Lord Je - sus Christ,
3. Lord Je - sus Christ,

Ky - ri - e e - lei - son. ___

you were sent to heal the con - trite, have mer - cy on us.
you came to call all sin - ners, have mer - cy on us.
you intercede for us at the right hand of the Fa - ther, have mer - cy on us.

O ___   O ___

47. AMEN

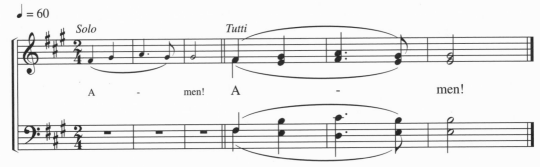

A - men! A - men!

48. GLORIA DEO

*Choose either part.

49. APOSTLES CREED

♩ = 72

Solo
I believe in God, the Father al-mighty, creator of heav-en and earth. A-men! A-men!

Tutti *Duo*
A-men! A-men! I believe in Jesus Christ, his only Son, our Lord.

He was conceived by the power of the Holy Spir-it and born of the Vir-gin Mar-y.

He suffered under Pontius Pi-late, was cru-ci-fied, and died, and was bu-ried.

He de-scended to the dead. On the third day he rose a-gain.

He a-scend-ed in-to heav-en, and is seated at the right hand of the Fa-ther.

Tutti
He will come again to judge the living and the dead. A-men! A-men! A-men! A-men!

Trio
I believe in the Holy Spirit, the holy, catholic, *(universal) church, the communion of saints,

the for-give-ness of sins, the res-ur-rec-tion of the bod-y

Tutti
and in life ev-er-last-ing. A-men! A-men! A-men! A-men!

* optional

50. SANCTUS DOMINUS DEUS

88

53. LORD'S PRAYER
(Traditional)

*optional

54. LORD'S PRAYER
(Contemporary)

Our Fa-ther in heav-en, ho-ly be your name. Your King-dom come.

Your will be done, on earth as in heav-en. Give us to-day our dai-ly bread.

For-give us our sins as we for-give those who sin a-gainst us.

* Keep us from temp-ta-tion, and de-liv-er us from e-vil.

For the King-dom, the pow-er and the glo-ry are yours, now and for-ev-er. A-men.

* optional

and de-liv-er us from e-vil. A - men.

55. AGNUS DEI–DONA NOBIS PACEM

English

56. PSALM 4: A DESIRE FILLS OUR BEING
Une soif emplit notre âme

A de - sire— fills our be - ing: to sur-ren-der all to you, O Christ.
U - ne soif em-plit no - tre â - me: nous a - ban-don-ner en toi, ô Christ.

Verses *(Cantor)*

The Lord hears when I call!
Tu m'é - cou - tes, Sei - gneur.

The Lord
Tu m'é -

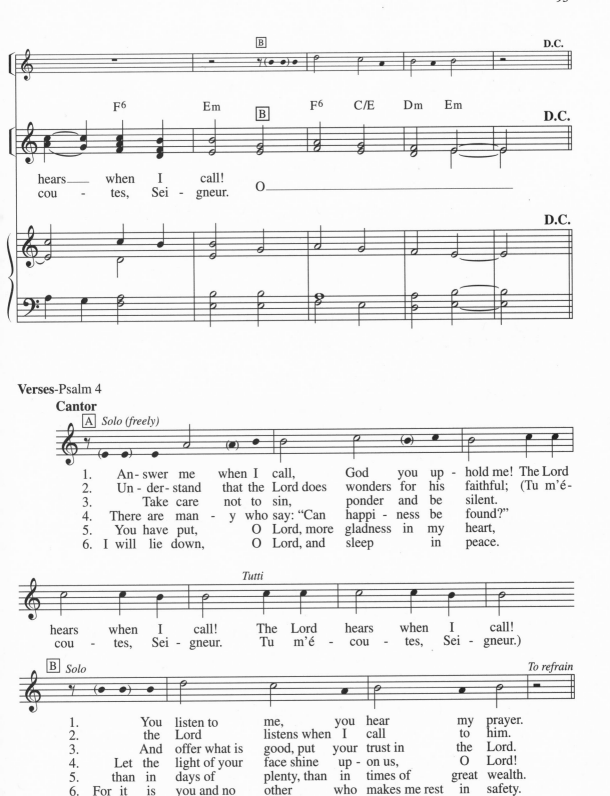

Verses-Psalm 4

Cantor

[A] *Solo (freely)*

1. An- swer me   when I call,   God   you up - hold me! The Lord
2. Un - der- stand that the Lord does wonders for his faithful; (Tu m'é-
3.   Take care not to sin,   ponder and be silent.
4. There are man - y who say: "Can happi - ness be found?"
5. You have put,   O Lord, more gladness in my heart,
6. I will lie down,   O Lord, and sleep   in peace.

Tutti

hears   when   I   call!   The   Lord   hears   when   I   call!
cou - tes, Sei - gneur.   Tu m'é - cou - tes, Sei - gneur.)

[B] *Solo*   *To refrain*

1.   You listen to me,   you hear   my   prayer.
2.   the Lord listens when I call   to   him.
3.   And offer what is good, put your trust in the Lord.
4. Let the light of your face shine up - on us, O Lord!
5. than in days of plenty, than in times of great wealth.
6. For it is you and no other   who makes me rest in safety.

57. PSALM 103: GOD CAN ONLY GIVE FAITHFUL LOVE

Dieu ne peut que donner son amour

God can on - ly— give faith-ful love: ten - der-ness and for - give - ness!
Dieu ne peut que don-ner son a-mour, no - tre Dieu est ten - dres - se!

Verses *(Cantor)*

God ev - er car - ing.
Dieu est ten - dres - se.

God ev - er car - ing.
Dieu est ten - dres - se.

Verses-From Psalm 103

Cantor

1. God can on-ly give faith-ful love.
2. Bless the Lord, O my soul,
3. The Lord for-gives all of your sins,
4. The Lord gives jus-tice for all who are op-pressed,
5. As the heav-ens are high a-bove the earth,

Our God ev - er caring. God ev-er car-ing.
all that is with-in me bless God's ho-ly name. (Dieu est ten-dres-se.)
and heals your wound-ed heart.
and makes known his ways to his people.
so great is God's stead-fast love.

1. God can on-ly give faith-ful love.
2. Bless the Lord, O my soul,
3. God re-deems your life from the grave,
4. The Lord is merci-ful and gracious,
5. As far as the east is from the west

God who for-gives us. God who for-gives us.
and do not for-get God's good deeds. (Dieu qui par-don-ne.)
and crowns you with love and mercy.
a-bounding in stead-fast love.
so far God re-moves our sins from us.

58. PSALM 62: IN YOU OUR HEARTS FIND REST

En tout, la paix du cœur

Verses *(Cantor)*

My hope is in the Lord.
De lui, vient mon es-poir!

Verses-From Psalm 62

Cantor

1. For God a - lone my soul waits in silence,
2. For God a - lone my soul waits in silence,
3. Trust in God at all times,
4. Do not put your trust in hu - man might,
5. For God has said on - ly one thing,

Tutti (My

from God comes my sal - vation.
for my hope is in the Lord.
trust in God, you, his people!
nor vain hopes in re - venge.
twice have I heard:

hope is in the Lord)

1. God a - lone is my rock, my sal - vation,
2. On God rests my sal - vation and my glory;
3. Pour out your heart be - fore the Lord;
4. Do not set your hearts on riches
5. that strength be - longs to God a - lone,

To refrain

my stronghold, I stand firm.
my refuge is the Lord.
for God is our refuge.
even when they in - crease.
to you, Lord, faith - ful love.

59. PSALM 145: THERE CAN BE NO GREATER LOVE

Grande est ta bonté

(John 15:13 para.)

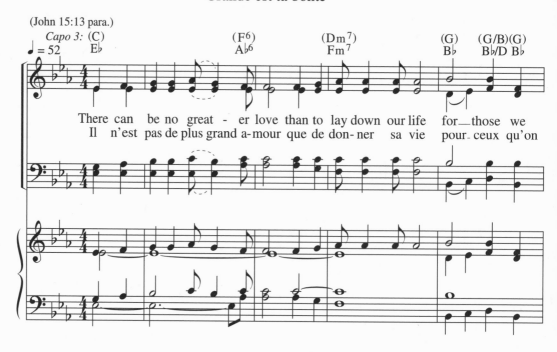

There can be no great - er love than to lay down our life for — those we
Il n'est pas de plus grand a-mour que de don- ner sa vie pour ceux qu'on

Verses *(Cantor)*

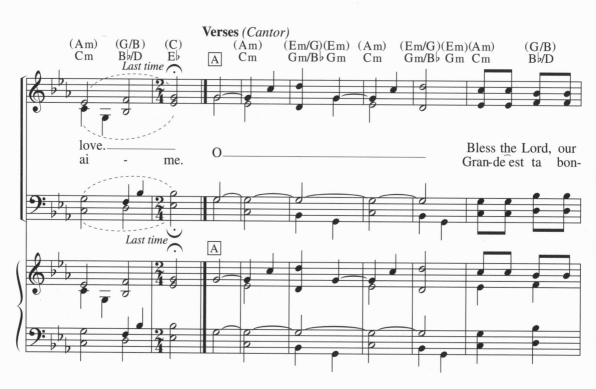

love.
ai - me.

O

Bless the Lord, our
Gran-de est ta bon-

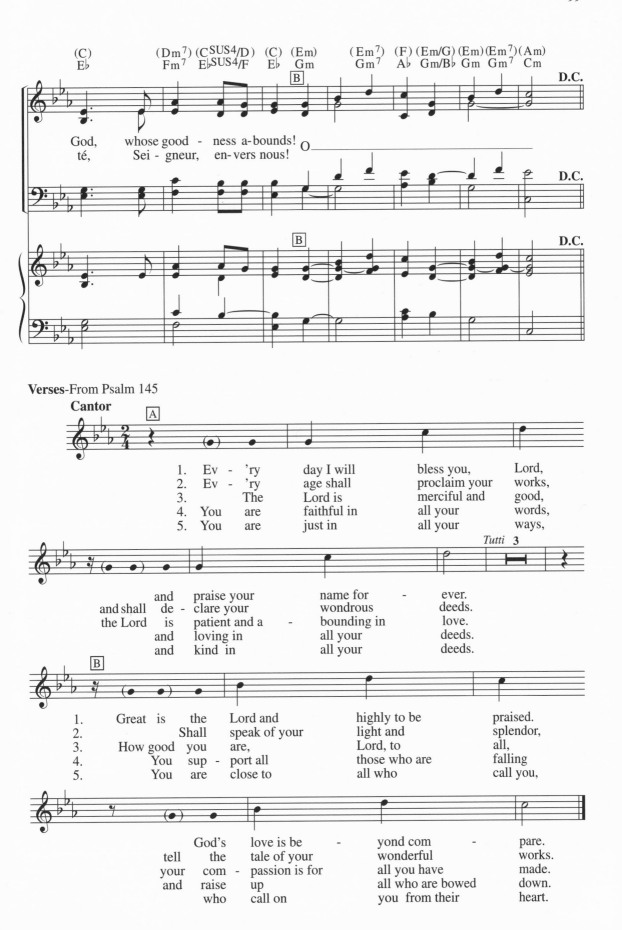

God, whose good - ness a-bounds! O_____
té, Sei - gneur, en - vers nous!

Verses-From Psalm 145

Cantor

1. Ev - 'ry day I will bless you, Lord,
2. Ev - 'ry age shall proclaim your works,
3. The Lord is merciful and good,
4. You are faithful in all your words,
5. You are just in all your ways,

Tutti 3

and praise your name for - ever.
and shall de - clare your wondrous deeds.
the Lord is patient and a - bounding in love.
and loving in all your deeds.
and kind in all your deeds.

1. Great is the Lord and highly to be praised.
2. Shall speak of your light and splendor,
3. How good you are, Lord, to all,
4. You sup - port all those who are falling
5. You are close to all who call you,

God's love is be - yond com - pare.
tell the tale of your wonderful works.
your com - passion is for all you have made.
and raise up all who are bowed down.
who call on you from their heart.

Topical Index

The numbers given after the selections in the Topical, Scriptural, and Language Indexes are item numbers, not page numbers.

THE LITURGICAL YEAR

Advent
In te confido   9
Our Soul Is Waiting   19
Wait for the Lord   30

Christmas
Christe Jesu lumen cordium   39
Gloria II canon   34
Nunc dimittis   16

Lent
Adoramus te, O Christe   38
Bless the Lord   3
De noche iremos   5
Exaudi nos   40
Our Darkness   18
Sing to the Lord   22
Venite, exultemus Domino   29
Your Word, O Lord   32

Holy Week
Adoramus te, O Christe   38
All You Who Pass This Way   1
Eat This Bread   7
Jesus, Remember Me   11
Oculi nostri   17
Psalm 145: There Can Be No Greater Love   59
Ubi caritas Deus ibi est   25

Triduum
Adoramus te, O Christe   38
Eat This Bread   7
Jesus, Remember Me   11
Maranatha! Alleluia! I   43
Oculi nostri   17
Ubi caritas Deus ibi est   25

Easter
Be Not Afraid   2
Bless the Lord   3
Christus resurrexit   4
Eat This Bread   7
In te confido   9
Jubilate cœli   35
Laudate Dominum   12
Maranatha! Alleluia! I   43
Psallite Deo   20
Surrexit Christus   23
Surrexit Christus (Gloria II canon)   34
Surrexit Dominus vere II   36

Pentecost
Come and Pray In Us (Gloria II canon)   34
Tui amoris ignem   24
Veni Creator Spiritus   26
Veni Creator Spiritus (Gloria II canon)   34
Veni lumen   27
Veni lumen cordium I   44

Veni lumen cordium II   45
Veni Sancte Spiritus   28

General
Bless the Lord   3
Eat This Bread   7
Lord Jesus Christ   15
Sing to God   21
Sing to the Lord   22
Ubi caritas Deus ibi est   25
With You, O Lord   31

RITES OF THE CHURCH

Baptism
With You, O Lord   31

Confirmation
Come and Pray In Us (Gloria II canon)   34
Oculi nostri   17
Sing to God   21
Tui amoris ignem   24
Veni Creator Spiritus   26
Veni Creator Spiritus (Gloria II canon)   34
Veni lumen   27
Veni lumen cordium I   44
Veni lumen cordium II   45

Eucharist
E. Eucharist   46-55
Eat This Bread   7
Ubi caritas Deus ibi est   25

Funeral
Be Not Afraid   2
Bless the Lord   3
Da pacem, Domine   33
Dona nobis pacem   6
Eat This Bread   7
In te confido   9
Jesus, Remember Me   11
Nunc dimittis   16
Our Soul Is Waiting   19
With You, O Lord   31

Marriage
Bless the Lord   3
Lord God, You Love Us   14
Our Soul Is Waiting   19
Ubi caritas Deus ibi est   25

Healing
Veni lumen   27
Your Word, O Lord   32

Penance
Bless the Lord   3
In God Alone My Soul   8
In The Lord I'll Be Ever Thankful   10
Our Darkness   18

TOPICAL

Alienation

Blessing

Comfort

Compassion

Confidence

Discipleship

Eternal Life

Evening

Faith

Forgiveness

Gentleness

Healing

Holy Spirit

Hope

Jesus Christ

Kingdom

Scriptural Index

Language Index

Taizé Recording Index

This index shows where to find the pieces in this volume on all of the available Taizé recordings from GIA. The numbers listed after the piece indicates the specific recording on which it may be found. For example, "Eat This Bread 9" is found on recording #9, "Wait for the Lord."

Taizé Recordings

1. Joy On Earth! CD/CS-443
2. Ubi Caritas CD/CS-399
3. Sing to God CD/CS-380
4. Veni Sancte Spiritus CD/CS-325
5. Jubilate CD/CS-284
6. Songs and Prayers from Taizé CD/CS-266
7. Canons and Litanies CS-203
8. Cantos de Taizé CS-201
9. Wait for the Lord CD/CS-173
10. Alleluia CD/CS-194
11. Taizé: Cantate CS-156
12. Resurrexit CS-169
13. Taizé in Rome CS-157

Musical Items

A. Ostinatos and Responses
3. Bless the Lord   3, 6, 10
4. Christus resurrexit   2, 8, 12
5. De noche iremos   8, 10
7. Eat This Bread   9
8. In God Alone My Soul   3, 12
9. In te confido   3, 4
10. In the Lord I'll Be Ever Thankful   3, 6, 10
11. Jesus, Remember Me   3, 5
12. Laudate Dominum   1, 5, 6, 8, 13
13. Let Us Sing to the Lord   3, 5
14. Lord God, You Love Us   3, 4
15. Lord Jesus Christ   3, 5
16. Nunc dimittis   1
18. Our Darkness   12
19. Our Soul Is Waiting   1, 5
20. Psallite Deo   1, 6, 8, 9, 12
21. Sing to God   3, 5
23. Surrexit Christus   8, 9, 12
24. Tui amoris ignem   3, 4
25. Ubi caritas Deus ibi est   1, 2
26. Veni Creator Spiritus   3, 5, 7
27. Veni lumen   3, 4
28. Veni Sancte Spiritus   1, 4, 6, 7, 8, 11, 13
30. Wait for the Lord   1, 6, 9, 10
32. Your Word, O Lord   3, 4

B. Canons
33. Da pacem, Domine   4
34. Gloria II, Cantate Domino,
      Veni Creator Spiritus canon   2, 7, 10
35. Jubilate cœli   1, 4
36. Surrexit Dominus vere II   1, 7, 11

C. Acclamations
37. Alleluia
    Alleluia 1   4
    Alleluia 8   3
    Alleluia 10   5
    Alleluia 17   1
    Alleluia Zagorsk   2, 4

D. Litanies
38. Adoramus te, O Christe   1, 11
40. Exaudi nos   7, 12
41. Gospodi
    Gospodi A   5
    Gospodi B   6
    Gospodi E   4
42. Kyrie eleison
    Kyrie 6   8
    Kyrie 9   13
    Kyrie 17   1
43. Maranatha! Alleluia! I   11
44. Veni lumen cordium I   12

E. Eucharist   1, 2

G. Psalms
56. Psalm 4: A Desire Fills Our Being   2
57. Psalm 57: God Can Only Give Faithful Love   2, 3
59. Psalm 145: There Can Be No Greater Love   1, 2